THE COOLEST JOBS ON THE PLANET

Animator

Tom Bancroft with Nick Hunter

Raintree

Chicago, Illinois

Edited by Andrew Farrow, Christine Peterson, and
Helen Cox Cannons
Designed by Cynthia Akiyoshi
Original illustrations © Capstone Global Library Limited 2014
Illustrated by HL Studios
Picture research by Mica Brancic and Tracy Cummins
Production by Helen McCreath
Originated by Capstone Global Library Limited
Printed and Bound in the United States Of America by
Corporate Graphics

18 17 16 15 14
10 9 8 7 6 5 4 3 2 1

Library of Congress Cataloging-in-Publication Data
Bancroft, Tom, author.
 Animator : the coolest jobs on the planet / Tom Bancroft and
Nick Hunter.
    pages cm. — (The coolest jobs on the planet)
 Includes bibliographical references and index.
 ISBN 978-1-4109-6640-7 (hb) — ISBN 978-1-4109-6646-
9 (pb) 1. Animators—Juvenile literature. 2. Animation
(Cinematography)—Vocational guidance—Juvenile literature. I.
Hunter, Nick, author. II. Title.

 TR879.5.B36 2015
 741.5'8023—dc23   2013040698

Acknowledgments
We would like to thank the following for permission to
reproduce photographs: We would like to thank the following for
permission to reproduce photographs: Alamy pp. 19 (Moviestore
collection Ltd/©1991 Disney), 20 (Photos 12/Walt Disney
Pictures/©1994 Disney), 22 (Image Source Plus/IE164),
26 (Jeff Morgan 06), 35 (AF archive/©1998 Disney);
©Disney p.10; Getty Images pp. 4 (uniquely india), 13 bottom
(Ron Galella Collection), 16 (Archive Photos/Earl Theisen
Collection/©Disney), 24 (WireImage/Richard Bord/©Disney),
25 (Paul A. Hebert), 31 (MAX NASH/AFP), 37 (E+/Steve
Debenport), 38 (Gamma-Rapho/Remi BENALI), 40 (Image
Source/davidgoldmanphoto), 41 (David McNew); Rex Features
pp. 7 (Everett Collection/CSU Archives), 23 (courtesy Everett
Collection/Walt Disney Pictures/©2013 Disney/Pixar), 27 (Snap
Stills), 32 (Sipa Press); Shutterstock pp. 6 magazines (Aleksei
Gurko), 13 top (Sergio Schnitzler), 15 (wdeon), 21 lion (Maggy
Meyer), 33 (Lucky Business); Tom Bancroft pp. 5, 8, 9, 11, 12,
14, 17 (©Disney), 18, 21 right, 28, 29 (©Disney), 30, 34
(CharConcepts), 36, 37 top, 39. Design elements Shutterstock.

Cover photo of Tom Bancroft sketching a character and other
animated characters reproduced with permission of Tom Bancroft.

Every effort has been made to contact copyright holders of
material reproduced in this book. Any omissions will be rectified in
subsequent printings if notice is given to the publisher.

All the Internet addresses (URLs) given in this book were valid at
the time of going to press. However, due to the dynamic nature
of the Internet, some addresses may have changed, or sites may
have changed or ceased to exist since publication. While the author
and publisher regret any inconvenience this may cause readers, no
responsibility for any such changes can be accepted by either the
author or the publisher.

Contents

On the Big Screen

You've been waiting weeks for this moment. The latest animated feature film is showing at the movie theater in your town. You've already seen the trailer. The movie's characters, with voices by your favorite actors and actresses, seem to be everywhere from toys to TV commercials. As the lights go down, you prepare to be amazed by the colorful and entertaining characters that dance across the screen.

After working on an animated film for years, finally getting to hear an audience laughing at it is a great feeling.

Behind this amazing visual experience are hundreds of people, including animators like me. My name is Tom Bancroft, and I've helped to create many successful films and characters. I helped animate the Disney movie *Mulan*, and I can remember seeing it on the big screen for the first time. I had worked on creating the character of the dragon, Mushu. It made all the hard work worthwhile when I heard the audience laughing at the scenes that I had devoted many months to creating.

TOOLS OF THE TRADE: WHAT IS AN ANIMATOR?

The job of animators is to create the moving pictures and characters in animated films. They do this by creating thousands of individual pictures that appear to move when shown in quick succession. Animators use skill and imagination to show things that would be impossible in a live-action film using actors. They create scenes and characters that are real enough to be believed, loved, or hated by an audience.

Animators use their drawing skills to show the emotions and personality of each character, as I have done here.

Cartoon Crazy

I was born and grew up in Inglewood, California. Like many children, I was captivated by the cartoons I saw on TV and at the movies. In the 1970s, there were no DVDs or Internet. If you wanted to see the latest movies, you had to buy a ticket to see them at a movie theater.

I have always loved superhero comic books for their exciting stories and dynamic drawings. I have studied anatomy my entire career because of the drawings I have seen in comic books.

Although I loved animation, I knew little about how it was made. I knew that the comic strips in newspapers were drawn by artists, so that was my first inspiration to start drawing myself.

Early inspirations

My biggest inspiration was the *Peanuts* comic strip drawn by
Charles Schulz. The comic strip showed how a skilled artist
could create complex characters with real emotions. I also loved
superhero comic books featuring characters such as Spider-Man
and The Avengers. I could see that the drawing skills needed to
create these comic books were much more advanced than I could
match at that stage. If I was going to reach that level, I would
have to draw all the time and improve my skills.

My hero!
Charles Schulz [1922-2000]

Peanuts is one of the most successful comic strips of all time. It is read by more
than 350 million people in thousands of newspapers. Schulz drew the comic strip
and its cast of characters, including Charlie Brown and his dog, Snoopy, from 1950
until his death in 2000. Even successful artists like Schulz had to deal with failure:
his early drawings were rejected by his high school yearbook.

Learning my trade

My twin brother, Tony, and I were fascinated by animation. We knew that the only way to develop our skills was to draw as much as possible. During our teenage years, we drew our own cartoons and comic strips whenever we could.

Tony and I were very competitive, but we also learned a lot from commenting on each other's work. If you want to improve at something, it is always important to have someone you trust to give honest views on your work.

CRUSADER

November 24, 1982

...AND UNEMPLOYMENT WASN'T EVEN ONE OF MY CAMPAIGN PROMISES!

This is an early comic strip that Tony and I drew for our high school newspaper. We used to sign the artwork we did together as "T&T" because we thought it sounded like dynamite!

NOTE TO SELF

If you have ever made a flipbook on the side of one of your books, then you have created animation! Professional, traditional animation is the same idea — just with bigger paper and many more people working on it.

In the days before the Internet, it was more difficult to make contact with professional artists. However, we were able to contact several professional artists who gave us advice on our work and how to get noticed. You should always be careful when making contact with people you don't know and make sure an adult knows what you're doing before you arrange to meet anyone.

TOOLS OF THE TRADE: PENCILS

You don't need any expensive equipment or software to start developing your animation skills. I normally use a simple blue or red pencil to create rough outlines and then a soft 2B pencil to complete the drawing. You can easily rub out the blue and red marks. It is often possible to remove them from a scanned image using image-editing software, which allows you to select all marks in a particular color.

This is an early photograph of my twin brother, Tony, at his first desk. I had the same desk and looked the same as him, too—in fact, I think that was my shirt that he's wearing in this photo!

The world of animation

Animation is all about making still objects or pictures look like they are moving. My career has mostly been spent in traditional animation. Traditional animators make films by creating a series of still drawings that become a moving picture when they are shown one after the other very quickly. Other forms of animation work on the same idea, but the pictures are made in different ways, as we will see.

©Disney

Did you know?

When you watch a film, each second includes 24 different frames or pictures. Therefore, for each minute of film on-screen, animators have to create 1,440 frames. And that figure is if there is only one character in the scene: for each new character in a shot, the drawing count doubles!

Stop-motion

Stop-motion animation uses models or puppets, which are moved slightly for each different frame. Ray Harryhausen was a pioneer of this type of animation who inspired me when I was starting out. The Wallace and Gromit films of Nick Park and Aardman Animations are created using stop-motion animation with clay models. Park's early work was a great eye-opener for me, as the animation brought so much life to simple characters.

When I was at Disney, stop-motion animation legend Ray Harryhausen visited the studio and talked about his career. It was a thrill for me to meet him.

Computer animation

Since the 1980s, computers have had a huge impact on all areas of animation. In 1995, John Lasseter and Pixar produced *Toy Story*, the first animated feature film created entirely on computer. This showed that computers could be used to create believable characters. Computer animation techniques have also been widely used to create special effects in live-action films.

First Steps

In 1987, I went to the California Institute of Arts (CalArts) to study animation. Walt Disney founded the school in the 1960s. It was a great place to make contacts in the animation industry, although at the time my ambition was to draw comic strips.

My time at CalArts was important in helping me understand more about different illustration techniques. However, going to college did not give me all the skills I needed to succeed in the world of animation. There are far more people looking for a career in the animation industry than there are available jobs. If you want to get that dream animation job, hard work has always been just as important as talent.

This is me (left) and my brother, Tony, at CalArts. I'm showing off one of my drawings for the short film I was working on. Tony is eating peanuts!

Introduction to animation

One of my friends had created a stop-motion animation using clay models and a Super 8 motion picture camera (left). As I discovered more about animation techniques, I realized how I could use my drawing skills to create moving pictures.

Did you know?

In college, Tony and I became good friends with a fellow artist in art class named Eric Stefani. In addition to enjoying a successful career as a musician with his sister, Gwen Stefani, Eric went on to work as an animator on *The Simpsons*. There are a few shots where Eric put our last name into the backgrounds behind Homer and his family. One shot has a big billboard in the background of a city scene and it says "Bancroft Biscuits"!

Learning about characters

The character-design classes were some of my favorites in college, but I had now decided I wanted to be an animator. I was learning so much about different aspects of animation that it was difficult to stay focused on my goal. But it was my years of drawing that eventually led me toward the first step in my career.

That's me, at the bottom right, in our design class at CalArts. Our instructor, Bob Winquist, was one of the best in the business.

My big break

After my brother, Tony, and I had been studying at CalArts for just over a year, we heard some exciting news. The Walt Disney Company was looking for animation talent and would be coming to our college. Hopeful animators in art schools across the country would be trying to win one of the nine-week internships that Disney was offering. My brother and I were two of the lucky ones. I left college and started on my career as an animator.

TOOLS OF THE TRADE: GESTURE DRAWINGS

Disney was looking for artists who could capture an expression or movement of a character. The best way to practice these skills is to draw people in action, such as the movement of people playing volleyball. These are called gesture drawings, because the goal is to capture the flow and line of action of the pose. If your dream is to land a job in computer animation, employers may be more interested in how you animate, but gesture drawings will also help you.

NOTE TO SELF

I wish I had completed my degree, but it was not needed when I started in the industry. Degrees are important for many animation jobs, but the chance to work for Disney does not come along very often.

Making My Mark

Landing an internship at Disney was my big break. I had a few weeks to prove that I had the talent and the commitment to be successful at Disney. It was an exciting time, as animators were working on *The Little Mermaid* (1989). This movie would help to revive the fortunes of Disney, and traditional animation, just at the right time for me. I was offered a permanent job at the new Disney studio in Florida.

One of the women of the Ink and Paint Department reviews animation "cels" of Snow White. Cels were used in the traditional method of animation.

©Disney

My hero!
The Walt Disney Company

Disney has been the leading name in animation ever since Walt Disney produced *Steamboat Willie*, the first animated film with sound, in 1928. Since then, Walt Disney Animation Studios has produced many of the best-loved animated feature films, from *Snow White and the Seven Dwarfs* (1937) to *Frozen* (2013).

Cleaning up and filling in

No one walks into a big studio like Disney and becomes an animator right away. You have to earn the chance. The first step for most new recruits is "clean-up." The people in the clean-up department take the roughly drawn characters created by animators and trace over the outlines, so that the drawings are ready to be colored and have backgrounds added.

Another job for junior members of the animation team is working as an "inbetweener." Animators create the main pose drawings for the character's movement, but between these key moments there are several frames where a character's arm or leg moves slightly, or where the expression on the character's face changes. Filling in these gaps is the job of the inbetweeners. The inbetween drawings help smooth out the animator's animation and make it more graceful.

©Disney

These are four key drawings of mine from a scene I animated for the movie *Pocahontas*. An "inbetweener" would create new drawings (one or more) between each of these drawings to make the movement even more graceful.

Taking the test

I loved being part of an animation production, but while I was in clean-up, I began to want to animate my own characters. To move out of clean-up and into animation, you had to do animation tests to show that you had the talent to progress.

Junior animators spend a lot of their spare time doing animation tests. At Disney, this meant creating a new scene with an existing character and dialogue. One of my tests used Captain Hook from the Disney version of *Peter Pan* (1953). The test is all about creating a performance by the character to show what you can do.

This is a character of my own design, and here I am making an animation test of him running in place.

When there is a job available for an animator, the people in charge look at all the animation tests to decide who deserves a chance. Usually, there are only one or two entry-level animation positions per film, with about 30 people trying for them!

©1991 Disney

I became an animating assistant, or junior animator, on *Beauty and the Beast* (1991), but I was still a long way from doing close-up scenes of characters talking. I got bored doing "crowd scenes" on *Beauty and the Beast* during the day. I started drawing comics at night and on weekends for Disney comics.

Did you know?

Although I did not always enjoy my work on *Beauty and the Beast*, the

Aladdin (1992) was the first film in which I was able to create scenes where I was animating major characters, such as the villain, Jafar, and his parrot, Iago. Animators were usually assigned to specific sequences within the film, and then we would be given a chance to work on a character within that sequence. The characters themselves are designed by supervising animators.

During the 1990s, I worked on around 10 feature films, including *The Lion King* and *Pocahontas*. One of the best things about working as an animator is the new challenge that comes with each project.

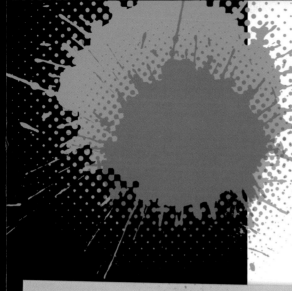

Mulan and Mushu

The traditional Chinese tale of *Mulan* was the first feature film to be completely animated in Disney's Florida studio, where I was working. It also gave me the chance to design a character of my own, the red dragon Mushu.

Did you know?

The character design and animation movement for *The Lion King* was helped by studying live animals brought to the studio! Watching, drawing, and touching real lions helped us capture their movements in a believable way, while we also added the fantastical element of having them talk and act like people.

Great Animator?

Walt Disney is said to have believed that it takes 10 years to make a good animator. When I started my career, this seemed like a very long time. However, I can now see that it took me many years before I really knew what I was doing.

If you want to be a great animator, you need to focus as much as you can on the areas described on these two pages. They are just as important for computer animation as they are for traditional animation.

Drawing

When people tell me they want to be animators, the first thing I ask is whether they draw every day. There really are no shortcuts. I studied the drawing styles of the best animators and illustrators I could find. This is the essential base for your work as an animator.

Performance

The other key skill for an animator is creating the action or performance. If you want people to love the animations you create, characters have to move smoothly and naturally. You have to study how people and animals move and make sure you transfer that to your animations. Actors have to make the parts they play believable, and you also have to do that using your animations.

You will always be working with a team of other animators responsible for their characters. Sometimes you are animating the same character as another animator. There cannot be multiple versions of the same character in the film, so being consistent is important.

©2013 Disney/Pixar

Disney/Pixar's *Monsters University* is a film that has lots of great examples of both subtle and broad performances by the characters.

NOTE TO SELF

Individual animators can do good animation, but great animation is always a group effort.

Great animation is all about the moments when everything comes together. It's about more than just the moving pictures, with story and voice actors helping to create a magical scene. The following people created some of the great animation that inspired me.

My hero!
Glen Keane [born 1954]

Glen Keane was a legend at Disney when I worked with him on *Pocahontas*. I saw firsthand the attention to detail and high standards that made him a key figure in the studio's successful films for the decade after *The Little Mermaid* (1989). Keane was also a pioneer of computer animation when he teamed up with John Lasseter to create a short test film of the book *Where the Wild Things Are* in the early 1980s. This was one of the first films to mix computer and traditional animation.

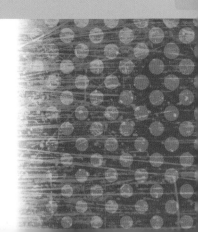

©Disney

My hero!

Milt Kahl [1909-1987]

The classic Disney animations from the 1940s to the 1960s were created by Walt Disney's team known as the Nine Old Men. Milt Kahl was probably the leading member of this group. He created some of the greatest characters in animation, including Shere Khan in *The Jungle Book* (1967).

My hero!
Mark Henn
[born 1958]

For much of my time at Disney, I worked closely with supervising animator Mark Henn, and I learned more from him than anyone else. Mark was the animator for some of Disney's most important lead characters, including Princess Jasmine in *Aladdin*. Mark was great to work with, but he was so talented and worked so fast that there were often not many exciting scenes left over for the other animators, like me, who worked with him.

Creating a Scene

When working on a feature film, animators typically work on a weekly schedule. Scenes are assigned at the start of the week. Our deadline for completing the scene is Friday of the same week, depending on the scene's length or complexity.

NOTE TO SELF

Remember, every scene is an opportunity to surprise the audience and move the story along, so there is always pressure to come up with something funny or creative.

On Monday, the directors give the animators as much information as they can, including how the scene should look and notes on the character's performance. A storyboard gives us a clear map of how each scene fits into the whole film.

TOOLS OF THE TRADE: DIALOGUE

One of the most important guides to creating a scene is the dialogue spoken by actors, which is recorded first. Often these actors are famous movie or TV stars, such as Eddie Murphy, who voiced the character Mushu that I created for *Mulan*. Animators study every word, listening over and over again to every emphasis and pause, to help them figure out the performance of the scene.

Planning

The first step is to make a plan of the scene. Which characters are involved and how will they move? Some scenes will involve very complicated action with lots of characters. Others may seem much calmer, but animators will still need to map out any change in the main characters' expressions or the small movements needed to make the scene realistic. I usually create small sketches called thumbnails to plan out the poses and acting of my characters.

Here, a voice actor is in a studio recording his performance for the movie *Smurfs 2*.

27

Creating the Frames

In traditional animation, once the scene is planned, the animator creates a rough outline of the key poses. It is not important to map out every frame of movement, as gaps will be filled by inbetweeners or the computer. The important things are to draw the characters accurately and to capture the key moments of the scene.

Once the director is happy, we will start to create the final drawings. Characters are drawn on separate sheets of paper, which are later scanned into the computer and combined with the painted backgrounds. Each frame can be made up of several layers of image, including the background, effects animation, shadows, and each character.

Notice that each character has its own set of drawings. But these would be combined in the computer so it looks like the characters are together in the scene.

An exposure sheet lists all the frames of the scene and matches them to the dialogue. There are 24 frames each second, so tiny mismatches between pictures and dialogue can cause a major problem. Once the scene is approved, the drawings are cleaned up and colored, ready to be captured on film.

Continuity

Although each scene is created separately, they all have to work together in the end. This is called continuity. I may be animating a scene where a character runs out the door, but if the character put a coat on in the scene before mine, I had better draw him wearing that coat now!

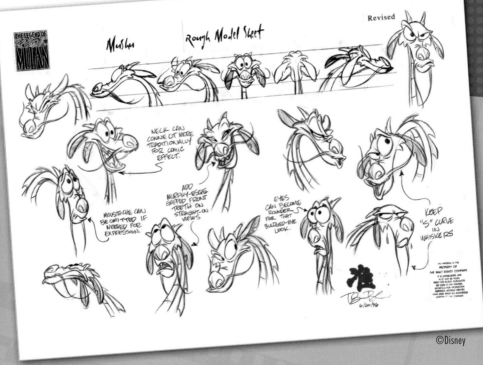

©Disney

Supervising animators are given the job of creating the design of the most important characters, but they would never be able to create every scene that included those characters. Model sheets are created to brief every animator on how to draw and animate characters, from the way they walk to how their eyebrows move when they are surprised.

Teamwork and Technology

Working for one of the big animation studios means that you are always working with a large team of people, often for months at a time. Teamwork is essential.

Each animated feature film is created by as many as 50 animators. In addition, there may be 200 or more people working on clean-up and as inbetweeners. Other people involved include background painters and layout artists. In total, there can be 500 to 800 people working to create thousands of frames for each film.

Animation studios, like this computer animation studio in Tennessee, are fun but busy, with lots of communication between animators needed.

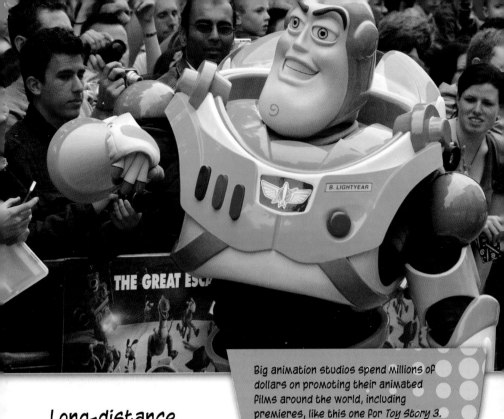

Big animation studios spend millions of dollars on promoting their animated films around the world, including premieres, like this one for *Toy Story 3*.

Long-distance animation

Tony and I have both worked on many of the same films, but not from the same place! He was based in California, and I was at the Florida studio. On *The Lion King*, we worked on the same sequence together, animating different characters. We shipped the drawings across the country for the next person to do his part! Once shot together, you couldn't tell that the same person hadn't animated the entire scene.

TOOLS OF THE TRADE: VIRTUAL STUDIO

Today, animation can be sent and shared via online "cloud" services that store large files. Video conferencing makes communication instant. More and more of the large studios are working with artists all over the world. I can work on a TV series via a "virtual studio," meaning there is no single studio building. Everyone works from home.

Working with technology

Traditional animation is still produced in a relatively low-tech way, although computers have made it much easier to get the timing exactly right between different frames and copy parts of the frame for use elsewhere.

Today's animated films are often produced using computer-generated imagery (CGI). The character designs and background environments are still hand drawn by artists, but then they are re-created (or "modeled") in the computer using digital modeling software.

Computer animators can record how real actors move and use this motion-capture technology to create animated effects.

Once the characters have been modeled, they are given complex skeletons (or "rigs") so that they can be manipulated at all the joints and muscles to create a performance. At this point, the animation process is very similar to stop-motion animation, where the CGI character "puppet" is moved slightly from pose to pose. Unlike traditional animation, though, the computer will fill in the frames between the key poses that the animator creates. CGI technology can also be used to create realistic special effects in live-action films.

Some films combine computer animation with the warm style of traditional character animation. Digital animation can create more realistic lighting, shadows, and movement. Fans of traditional animation argue that much of the art of animation is lost in this form.

TOOLS OF THE TRADE: COMPUTER ANIMATION TECHNOLOGY

The rise of affordable computer animation technology means that anyone with talent and a story to tell can produce animation on a home computer. These animations may not be as polished as the big-budget studio productions, but they offer animators a way to develop their skills. There are also more outlets for animation on web sites, apps, and video games.

Creating Characters

Audiences have always been attracted by characters that are funny and believable. The animator has to keep this in mind, whether the character is a child, a dragon, or even a car.

Throughout my career, taking the lead in designing characters is what I've enjoyed most. When I first designed the character Mushu for *Mulan*, I started working on the film almost a year before most of the animation team got involved. The directors introduced me to the story and characters, and then I had to come up with a design.

PIRATE GIRL

V.1   V.2

PIRATE BOY

V.1   V.2

Exploration is important to character design, so I draw many different versions of characters to show to directors or clients. Here are different versions of two pirate kid characters I created for a client.

At first, you are just creating one version of the character after another until the directors are happy. A character designer asks himself or herself lots of questions before even putting pencil to paper. Is the character a hero or a villain? What is the character's personality like? The job of the character designer is to express all these things in the pictures on the screen. This is a bit like what an actor does in a live-action film, except the animator may be able to use color, shape, and talking animals to get the message across.

©1998 Disney

Once the design is agreed upon, the character is put through animation tests to pin down every aspect of the character's poses, movement, and personality. The supervising animator then creates the model sheet for other animators to use when drawing the character.

NOTE TO SELF

The character Mushu talked like a human but was a dragon, so one of the most important things was for him to move like a fantastical character, or something you haven't seen before, not like a person in a dragon suit.

Animator at large

In 2000, I left Disney. This gave me the chance to work on many different film and TV animation projects for other studios, large and small. I also started a development art company with a friend. Funnypages Productions gave me the chance to work on the huge variety of projects I'd missed when I was a small part of a big studio. I created animation, storyboards, comic books, and children's book illustrations. The common thread to all these things was the chance to develop characters and tell stories.

This is a small sample of books I've illustrated over the years. I'm most proud of my two character design instructional books (at the front here).

Character Mentor

I also became interested in teaching others how to design characters and wrote a book called *Creating Characters with Personality* (2006). There are lots of books telling you how to draw and animate. I thought this was an area that young animators could learn more about. I have since written another book called *Character Mentor*. After 25 years working in animation, I still love designing new characters and advising up-and-coming young artists and animators.

Another great thing about working for myself is that I can live wherever I want. I currently live in Nashville, Tennessee, with my family, far away from the big animation studios!

TOOLS OF THE TRADE: RESEARCH

If you want to create realistic characters, you can't draw every expression or pose from memory. Don't be afraid to look on the Internet or in books to find the pose you want. You need to make sure that you take inspiration but do not copy anyone else's work. Looking in the mirror is another great way to see how different expressions look.

What's Next?

My job has changed a lot during my career. In most jobs, you try to focus more of your time on the parts you love doing. Most of my time is now spent on designing characters rather than on animation. I am head of character design for a TV program, creating characters that are then animated by a team in China.

When I first started in animation, there were not many options apart from traditional animation. Since then, clay animation and computer-generated animation have really taken off. CGI animation has changed the industry dramatically. Many film companies no longer use traditional animation.

Merchandising of popular characters from films gives people all over the world the chance to surround themselves with a character YOU may have helped bring to life!

NOTE TO SELF

You don't have to restrict yourself to one thing. I still love drawing comic strips. Now I can draw comic strips and post them online for people to see.

My comic strip *Outnumbered* is loosely based on my life with a family of all girls—my wife and four daughters!

Tom Bancroft

Outnumbered

AH, FOLDING LAUNDRY IS LIKE HAVING A "DON'T BOTHER DAD" FORCE FIELD.

FOOTBALL IS BORING. I WANT TO WATCH "CELEBRITY DANCE-OFF".

NO PROBLEM, MEGAN. YOU JUST HAVE TO HELP ME FOLD CLOTHES.

FORCE FIELD SET TO "MAXIMUM"!

www.OUTNUMBEREDCOMIC.com

COPYRIGHT 2013 TOM BANCROFT, ALL RIGHTS R

Like many traditional animators, I learned to do computer animation, but I missed drawing, which is what brought me to animation in the first place. I learned that computer animation still needs strong characters. I have found that I can use my drawing abilities and knowledge of animation to create character designs, storyboards, and other development art that works really well for CGI or traditional animation.

TOOLS OF THE TRADE: CG CHARACTERS

I now create characters in two dimensions with pencil and paper. These are used to create computer-generated models of my characters. Computers are fantastic tools for creating animated films, but they are only tools. Even the most advanced computer animation relies on great stories and characters.

animation means that the struggle to get a job in traditional film animation is fiercer than ever. But don't despair—many of the biggest blockbusters are created by animators. There are also a growing number of TV channels looking to make animated programs. Most TV series animation is created using traditional animation, so drawing is still a very important skill.

No matter how good your drawing or animation skills are, you'll still need to study hard at other subjects to get into the best colleges.

Practice and planning

If you want to get involved in animation now, you need to keep working on your drawing and animation skills. You should also look at colleges that offer animation classes. Find out what subjects and degrees you will need to give yourself the best chance in the future.

If you love the idea of making characters move and act to tell a story, then you should become a computer animator. If it is drawing and designing characters that drives you, then you may want to become a storyboard artist or a character designer. If you like both, like me, then do your best to be as good as you can at both; it will give you more opportunities to land your dream job.

TOOLS OF THE TRADE: APPS AND VIDEO GAMES

The world of animation has now spread far beyond the movie or TV screen. Animated films can be viewed online, but high-quality animation is also an essential feature of many apps and video games. Gamers expect characters and settings that are realistic, scary, or funny just as much as moviegoers do. This has created many opportunities for the animators who can create those characters.

Quiz

Do you have what it takes to become an animator? Take this quiz to find out.

1. What do you always carry around with you?

a) A video game console so I can play games wherever I am

b) A notebook so I can take notes and write stories

c) A sketchbook and pencils so I can draw the world around me

2. What do you want your career path to be like?

a) I want to be earning lots of money and have a big, fancy office with a view

b) I want a job that gives me lots of time off for relaxing and watching TV

c) I want to work in an industry that is fiercely competitive and gives me new challenges every day

3. What would give you the most satisfaction?

a) Earning lots of money to buy fast cars and an amazing home

b) Working on my own so I know that whatever I achieve is all my own work

c) Being part of a large team producing creative products that entertain millions of people

4. How would you describe your personality?

a) Steady – I like to follow established processes

b) Relaxed and laid-back

c) Creative and full of ideas

5. What do you like to do when playing on a computer?

a) Share photos and chat with friends

b) Play games

c) Create and edit my own art or films

If you answered mostly Cs, then you may be just the right kind of person to succeed in the animation industry.

Glossary

anatomy bodily structure of humans, animals, and other living things

cel (short for "celluloid") transparent sheet on which character drawings used to be reproduced in traditional animation. It is sometimes known as cel animation.

clean-up part of the animation process in which clean-lined versions of rough drawings are produced

comic strip series of drawings, often with speech bubbles, that appears in comics and newspapers

computer-generated imagery (CGI) images and animations created using a computer

continuity consistency in character, story, places, and other aspects of a film

dialogue conversation, particularly when written down and spoken by a character in a play or film

director creative person, with a vision of the film, who gives direction to the team making the film

exposure sheet tool that enables an animator to organize frames and give instructions on how a scene should be shot; also called an X-sheet

feature film film that is long enough to make up the main part or all of a presentation at a movie theater, usually lasting 80 minutes or longer

frame single image in a strip of film. Those photographed frames are then spooled through a projector at fast speeds to create the illusion of movement. There are 24 frames per second in a standard film.

inbetweener animator who completes frames showing movements between important, or key, frames

internship temporary work with a company in order to gain experience

live action film that is made with real actors and is not animated

model sheet guide created by an animator that details all aspects of a character and shows the character from all angles and with every emotion

scene section of a film or play that usually takes place in a single setting and lasts a few seconds or minutes

stop-motion animation oldest form of animation, created by moving models and photographing each movement one frame at a time so it looks like the model is moving on its own

storyboard series of pictures outlining the story of a film or TV program, much like a very long comic strip

trailer short film designed to introduce highlights of a feature film and encourage people to go see it

Find Out More

Books

Animation (The Archive series). New York: Disney, 2009.

Bancroft, Tom. *Character Mentor*. Burlington, Mass.: Focal, 2012.

Bancroft, Tom. *Creating Characters with Personality*. New York: Watson-Guptill, 2006.

Both of my books listed here are aimed at animation students, but they contain examples for creating your own character designs.

Bancroft, Tony. *Directing for Animation: Everything You Didn't Learn in Art School*. Burlington, Mass.: Focal, 2014.

This is my twin brother's book. He talks about his experiences directing the film *Mulan* for Disney, and there are many interviews with other professional animation directors.

Bliss, John. *Art That Moves: Animation Around the World* (Culture in Action). Chicago: Raintree, 2011.

Levete, Sarah. *Make an Animation!* (Find Your Talent). Mankato, Minn.: Arcturus, 2012.

Lord, Peter, and Brian Sibley. *Cracking Animation*. New York: Thames and Hudson, 2010.

Williams, Richard. *The Animator's Survival Kit*. New York: Faber & Faber, 2009.

This is the best book about learning how to animate. It uses traditional animation (drawn) examples, but all the principles also relate directly to stop-motion or CG animation.

Web sites

www.aardman.com
This is the official web site of Aardman Animation.

www.disneyanimation.com
News and information about animated films from Disney can be found on this web site.

www.outnumberedcomic.com
This is my *Outnumbered* webcomic strip, which I do for fun. It's semi-autobiographical about my life with a wife and four daughters.

Topics for further research

There are lots of ways to discover more about the best in animation. There is an Oscar awarded every year for Best Animated Feature Film and Best Animated Short Film.

You can also find out more about key milestones in the history of animation from the early films of Walt Disney to modern computer animation created by studios such as Pixar, as well as the animators who created them.

Index

10 9 8 7 6 5